Lighting Upon
The Gita
At The Ganga

Lighting Upon The Gita At The Ganga

Radhika Vijay

Dedicated

To

"Lord Krishna & Guruji"

****

Foreword

"The Gita" is for The Old,

The highly spiritual and The Great Pandits,

and for sure , it is-

"NOT MY CUP OF TEA"

This is the beginning theme and thought of this book!

BUT

As you read along and get to know via my experience,

Your thoughts will be transformed into something like-

"The Gita" is for me, my kids and my whole family.

It is my guide in the darkness,

For my career and social dealings.

It is my financial and food guide.

If I am a student, Gita is for me.

If I am a teenager, a youngster,

It's my first spiritual guide and friend.

It is the solution to almost every struggle in the present.

It is my answer to every hurdle of the past

and YES, it is the hope and endurance for my beliefs

and unknown future queries, doubts and fears!

What is demanded of me is to have faith

and daily reading practice of this great Eternal scripture,

to be a proud Hindu and Indian and a responsible,

dutiful citizen of "Bharat".

I need to widen my horizons,

treat all with sympathy, empathy kindness

and equality and that is how I embrace

"The BhagavadGita" learnings

and commandments to adorn my life

and of those near me with love, compassion and

enlightenment!

You will agree once you wade through some wonderful,

helpful and some enlightening pieces of gen

and examples stated with enough certitude!

These will serve fringe benefits in

your ongoing speedy life,

your belief system and daily praxis.

****

Table Of Contents

****

Chapter 1
My Routine

My very "Normal Routine" is not the ideal one to be followed. It begins somewhat early in the morning since I have to catch my bus, I mean I have to rush to my duty or job , whatever you define it and being not late is really my joy!!

Next, my "Morning Routine" is a little spiritual and musical and thoughtful, reminding me about the most important goals of today, not the next day.

It is a kind of robotic effort of tickmarking the tasks like getting up, getting ready, milk boiling, breakfast preparation, getting kids ready for studies, etc.

Spiritual routines are very hasty like chanting Daily prayers, running to temple, and finally running to my workplace!

Many times, the spiritual routine is shortened to short prayers or prayer listening on mobile while travelling to the workplace.

Then there are seasons of fasting, yes I love to fast with great offerings to my Lords like Shivji, Ganeshji, Hanumanji, Mata Rani and many more. And like any other devotee, many times my Sankalpas are mightier than my efforts i.e. the beginnings are great while it becomes tough till the end of fasting routines. I try my best not to be at fault but it is well known- **"To Err is Human and to Forgive Is Divine"**.

And I assume that my Divine is kind to me, as I don't want to give thoughts of inefficiency and guilt for myself, simply to continue my routine as best as I can the next day!

That has been my concept and effort for my spiritual routine so far from many years now as I am balancing life, work, kid and my own self ●

Chapter 2
The Gifted Trip

Life was going on smoothly with occasional twists and turns and here I would like to share a tete-a-tete with all that I hardly travel and am a creature in my cocoon knitting up a creative holy corner of my own.

I have been thoroughly taught habits of godliness, cleanliness and kindness for mankind since my childhood. With roughness of working routines, it becomes extremely difficult to apply all these great habits but **"Knowledge is power"**

And I believe, some teachings take root in the semi conscious mind so nicely, that on your will, they can be easily withdrawn like cash from an ATM and used and applied easily wherever and whenever!

The mantra goes on like, "**Where there is a will, there is a way!**"

During tea time, one evening, I was mourning over my cancelled trip to HARIDWAR. It was nicely planned with my Mom and all bookings were made. My summer vacation coincided with my son's and it was all a dream trip. But due to some important domestic routines, My Mom urged me to cancel the whole trip and I was sipping hot tea over a heated argument with her.

My mourning continued for a few days as I daily watched the Ganga Arti over my Youtube and imagined myself sitting at the Ghaat and reliving the whole Sparkling Arti during evening hours.

One day I overheard My Aunt talking to my Mom about a Camp to be organised in Rishikesh, consisting of The Gita teachings and related activities like reading scriptures, practising Yoga and Pranayama and much more. She was actually planning to attend the Camp with my Mom and within a few days, all the things were finalised, forms were filled and registrations done, train bookings were done and they both were all set to attend the Camp.

But then, not to be mocked upon, "Aunts and Mommies have their own ways and gonna stay Aunts and Mommies only!"

Unbelievably, owing to their overwhelming upcoming Long time planned trips, they decided to cancel their Camp visit. Oh Yes, they did decide and very soon, I got to know about their recent trip modifications. I thought of myself as the benefited

Monkey amongst two cats. Surely the cats had no fight in this context. ●

As per Camp rules, there was no option of refund, and I offered my wish to visit Rishikesh in place of them. My vacations were going on and definitely, they had no arguments or thoughts against mine. And lo! Can you all imagine, I was given the gift of the trip from my Aunt and Mom to visit and attend the Camp in their replacement.

After the cancellation of my HARIDWAR trip, this was like a "Dream Come True" and I booked my tickets very soon, thought of accompanying my other Aunt from Delhi and travel plans were all Colouring my mind and thoughts like a "Rainbow" ◗

Chapter 3
Rishikesh

"**Google** is the best Friend in Need and A friend Indeed"

My trip search results began. I was looking for some weather predictions and also some worth visiting and worth eating spots in Rishikesh.

I had never been to Rishikesh and had always heard of it as a pretty, calm, holy place, an abode of Saints, Yogis and Devotees.

It was also referred to as the "Yoga Capital" of the country by one of the search results.

Geographically, it is situated in the foothills of the Great Himalayas in the North of Uttarakhand. And luckily it lies besides the Favourite and Great "River Ganga". Surely, that was my best reason to attend the Camp!!

There are numerous temples and Ashrams in the city for one's enlightenment and attainment of Spiritual Knowledge.

The one I was concerned with was "The Swarg Ashram"

I packed my camera, etc and all the stuff I could think of. Some suggestions were made by the Camp guidelines like one's own Asana, Mat, torch, lock, bedsheet, personal stuff, Chanting Mala and Gomukhi, etc.

I was very excited to visit the beautiful land of

Holiness and the River Ganga

Against the backdrop of Himalayas

The holy waters flowing within

Yoga Capital of the world

Wrapped in "Meditative Air"

Beautiful day Sceneries

Sunrise & Sunset paints the sky above & waters below

Heart of Traditions & Cultures

Abode of the Yogi & the Preachers

Nurturing land of our Culture

Innumerable holy hubs spread wide

One of which is going to be my abode for the next few days!

Rishikesh was Calling ●

Chapter 4
Swamiji's Guidance & Glory

"Without God's mercy, you cannot meet a True Saint"

That is an English translation of a verse from "The Ramcharitmanas"-

"Binu Hari Kripa Mile Nahi Santa"

Though I have a broken knowledge of verses from this great Hindu scripture, but I think, a few of them, I have crammed up like my books on Medical Sciences.

I am not so proud of this fact, but definitely happy to share these treasurable verses aptly in this book describing my emotions and feelings!

And I have no words to exactly define my experiences and feelings of knowing and meeting "Swamiji" (Swamiji Govind Dev Giri Ji Maharaj)

It was a mix of divine and eternal experience. The whole Camp was organised under his administration and his teachings on "The Gita" were deeply heartfelt and soulful discourses. Every vibration of the speech was a guiding light and enlightening precious pearl to be treasured and adopted forever!

My best encounters were with the descriptions of the Great - "The Bhagavad Gita". The teachings, or rather I should say the commandments of "The Gita" are truly marvellous and ought to be adopted and entwined in one's life, mind and thoughts strongly for achieving the best results!!

It was not "The Gita" only.

As you know well, the food is tasty not because of the ingredients and the recipe only, it is the charm, aura and glory of the Cook which finally defines the taste of the dish.

So is here,

The Magnetic Aura, Charm and Vibrant speech of "The Swamiji" was the driving force and factor that actually homed "The Gita" in everyone's mind, thoughts and soul.

It was no Ordinary discourse!

It was a magical wand which touched and not only promised but demanded true commitment and transformation from each and every true and dedicated devotee and listener.

"Magic was in the Air"

And who could be credited for this great, auspicious and heavenly atmosphere? No doubts, none other than "Swamiji"!

I designate him as "Guruji" ●

Chapter 5
My Learnings & Affirmations

Learnings of "The Gita" were compiled up during the whole Camp and many important points were laid emphasis on which were indispensable for day to day proper management and functioning of life while practising prayers, meditation and daily yoga or exercise.

It would be better to go in the manner adopted by "Swamiji" as nothing could strike the heads for better comprehension especially for the beginners and curious learners ●

- ***INTRODUCTION***

The sixth Chapter or Adhyaya of "The Gita"
is totally dedicated to teach self control. The
best way to progress and attain success via this
eternal scripture is to first and foremost calm
down one's inner self and be at pure peace and
no rebel inside!

If you remember the very famous Gayatri
mantra, it too emphasises on meditative and
peace attaining aspects.

There are 3 types of Yogas- the one via pure
intentions and Peace, second one via Asana
and Pranayama and third one via Meditation.
Well, it goes through the saying-"Sound mind
resides in a Sound body"

Our life can be made quite happy no matter
what is going on. Actually again it is to be

understood that "Happiness lies within yourself and not outside of yourself" Perceptions of mind need to be worked upon. It is not possible to read the great Vedas or Upanishads nor is it desirable to put time and effort in this direction. One should understand the fact that Vedas have their summary as Upanishads while Upanishads have their summary in "The Gita".

- ***ABOUT "THE GITA"***

One should know well enough that "The Gita" is not an essay or speech. It is in fact a "Dialogue" between Lord Krishna and Arjuna.

Arjuna is truly the apt listener of this Song of "The Gita"

The Gita explains beautifully that every work or deed done or undertaken is in fact a kind of Yagna/Yoga. So, according to this theory, the whole life of a person becomes a holy Yagna. And the condition is that the deed or work should be selfless and done for the benefit of mankind or humanity and should be offered to the Lord as a prayer.

Devotion (Bhakti) actually is through heart, soul, speech and deeds. It is a combination of all of these, then it is the true form of devotion.

- ***HOW TO STUDY/READ/COMPREHEND "THE GITA"?***

One should read "The Gita" or know "The Gita" or even one if bows down in respect or bestows his or her regards for "The Gita", nothing like it. All these dedications will be resulted in the blessings from "The Gita"

There should be wholehearted dedication and belief in the scripture and that is what all matters!

"The Gita" are the words of God, it is designated and I too believe, the best scripture in present times in the whole of the world!

This is not said in air or in vain. "The Gita" in fact fulfils all the necessary criterias that define the Value of a great scripture like Topic, the adopter or owner, the Result and the relation with the benefitted.

The whole sole purpose of "The Gita" is to define, find and identify the inner self God. When Arjuna asked, how will his all round development and progress occur, then Lord Krishna narrated "The Gita" for him.

You need to understand the right difference in the things or acts that you desire and the things or acts that are desired for your overall and ultimate benefit.

"Preyas" is your desire, while "Shreyas" is what is desired for you!

Till the person in front of you does not ask for a beneficial speech, please don't lecture anyone in vain. It would be a waste of your words, knowledge and efforts.

Always remember that the whole sole goal of "The Gita" is complete and all round benefit of mankind. This would be a state of total and immense satisfaction when no more desires breed in.

But I had already said that Arjuna was the truly apt listener for "The Gita". He fulfils all the qualities as he wishes and asks Lord Krishna the best way or remedy for his well being and complete benefit. And that is what Lord krishna wants to tell him in the form of "The Gita"

- ***LEARNINGS OF "THE GITA"***

"The Gita " begins and ends in offerings of oneself to God and seeking his protection and blessings. The best hand to hold is the hand of God no matter any difficulty you face in your life. "The Gita" is enriched with Values more than any other scripture. It is the scripture for everyone and for all life aspects.

Of course, it is too deep and wide to be fully understood but even a slight right knowledge of its pearls can prove valuable assets for one's life at any age- whether kids or middle grade students, college teenagers, uncles and aunts , parents, grandmas and grandpas.

Only requirement to adopt its preachings is to have a heart of gold, full of curiosity, compassion and the urge to learn more and more with full devotion and belief.

It is no doubt the best teacher of values, success, satisfaction in life, you need to have wide hearts and minds to space it all!

Two key elements of success in life are :

DISCIPLINE &

FOCUS/CONCENTRATION.

The key to focus and concentration is simplicity in life and practice of the truth.

It is always desirable to do actions and things liked by good hearted or saintly people and leave the actions or things desired or liked by evil hearted people.

The best way to concentrate is via practice of the control of food intake, taking the right healthy food and control of one's senses like what you see, listen, eat, think, like, etc. Eating the healthy food in the right quantity at the right time actually makes you fit and focussed for understanding the real learning and practising Asanas/Yoga in life.

Take enough sleep, do not oversleep and plan everyday in the morning early for your wins. Daily practice, exercise, Japa and good reading habits. One can read good holy scripture, quotes, sayings or life stories of the great people of the country, freedom fighters or saints. One should also cultivate an extra hobby apart from daily work/ essential chores to lead a stress free life.

- ***"THE GITA" GRANTS A KALEIDOSCOPIC GUIDANCE***

"The Gita" will guide you as per your wish and desire. It will guide a child, a student, a collegiate, a parent, a grandparent as per their wishes and desires.

One needs to practise discipline and self control to attain the maximum benefits. To be successful, develop the right and the good habits. Your good habits are your best friends and the reverse is true for your bad habits which will lead you into a dungeon! Make your own followable rules to develop good habits and start pursuing them without any delay. That is a sure step for success.

Students should make a daily routine checklist. Tick the right thing they did and cross the wrong thing or act they did. That is a kind of self check and evaluation. If the good deeds tick marks increase day by day, it's a sign one is on the right path to develop good habits and on the way to success.

Take time to learn and observe good and right deeds and things. Take time to chew food properly and eat only as per one's need not desire!

- ***"THE GITA" MESSAGE***

"The Gita" gives a great roadmap to Enlightenment!

As Lord Krishna sang "The Gita" amidst the warfield, so you can imagine that "The Gita" is simply ideal to derive all valuable pearls to achieve success and happiness in this Ultimate Struggle and Battlefield of Life!

It will guide you, Prepare you and make you a winner in this Life struggle.
Body is our tool, it is a machine, so we need to preserve and protect it by nurturing and nourishing it well enough to withstand the storms and rough weathers bestowed by time, destiny and situations upon us!

It is a prime responsibility to stay healthy and preserve our bodies for a happy, healthy and blessed long life!

One needs to make, plan, prepare and follow a special routine apt for oneself to achieve the aforesaid goal.

Take out time for all important tasks every day and plan deeply and nicely enough so that you get breaks and rest hours too. You need to find time for your family and your own self too!

Try eating seasonal fruits and veggies available locally to stay fit and healthy.

Cook food as per Indian recipes and eat a lot of variety of food.

Do exercise or Asana/Yoga daily. Create alone time for Japa and meditation to rejuvenate your inner self and peace and happiness.

Pursue some Pooja method or routine daily as per your time allows and practise it daily.

Never miss any task of your planned routine.

Slowly and steadily you will learn to master your time. Avoid sharing your Pooja tools like Japa string/Mala and Asana. These are your personal belongings.

Mind your speech too! Put up your right thoughts and opinions humbly and firmly!

Simplicity is the key to success.

Stay in the company of good and kind people.

To err is human, but don't hesitate to ask forgiveness and definitely do not repeat the mistakes again.

Leave laziness forever. God loves active, idealistic and happily working men and women doing each and every deed and thought in service with pure dedication to the Lord!

Little stress is good to achieve great progress as no stress will never let you progress or overcome your laziness. Step out of your comfort zone and see and make the Difference!

Note: All these teachings and extracts are borrowed from "Swamiji's" discourse and translated in simple English for easy comprehension!

Chapter 6
The River Ganga

The River Ganges

River Ganges, the symbol of beauty!

River Ganges, flowing waters so holy!

River Ganges, the pride of my culture!

River Ganges, the banks developed so eternal!

River Ganges, the point of my prayers!

River Ganges, I get to visit it really rare!

River Ganges, the source of traditions and themes!

River Ganges, fresh and cool water reserve always it seems!

My faith, devotion and regard only grows, never changes!

Whenever I get the wonderful opportunity to visit The River Ganges!!

Truly, these are my real feelings and perceptions as I stand by The Ganga Ghaat whether in Haridwar or Rishikesh (I have not visited any other city in fact)

In this section, I especially want to describe the Beautiful and Grand "Ganga Aarti" as I got the pleasure of living one while my stay in the Camp with the grace of "Swamiji"

You might have seen the beautiful Arti videos on Youtube or any other channel or link, but living it in person is simply the Grand and Eternal grace of God! It begins with pretty hymns and bhajans devoted to "The Ganga" and there are chanting of the Pooja, a lot of in Sanskrit, little tough to comprehend, but always pleasing and soothing to the ears.

Then time flies and the sun sets, it gets a little dark, you hold your pooja leafy vessel (dona) filled with flowers , incense sticks and Diya in honour to perform a perfect Arti of the River Ganga.

A little more dark, and everyone lights up their diyas, the lights everywhere shine up and illuminate the surroundings. All the faces are well lit with their Diyas and the Amazing Arti hymn begins. It is a super captivating and breath holding moment to live. You cannot take your eyes off the sparkling waters of the River Ganga. It is all diamond and golden. It does not look like normal waters, It becomes the mirror echoing and reflecting deeply rooted devotional feelings, thoughts, sounds and diyas held by everyone. The river Ganga becomes Alive! And you can actually feel the holy vibes flowing from "The Ganga" within your heart and soul!

Nothing stays in your heart but simply love,

devotion, praise and gratitude!

Such is the Great beautiful Arti of "The Ganga"

river.

I really wish you get a chance to attend one whenever

you next plan your trip to any of these mentioned

cities.

Chapter 7
Takeaway Message

So, it is the time of Takeaways.

Well! In this section I would just like to keep my words short and few points. Let us begin..

- "The Gita" is simply a great and wonderful Hindu (Indian) scripture for all-kids, young, parents, grandparents!

- The power and values of scriptures should not be underestimated based on their language (hindi or Sanskrit) and their presence from historical times.

- There is no generation gap or rule or criteria or ceremony to begin reading and understanding "The Gita". I too lighted upon this Eternal literary scripture into oblivion.

- I specially emphasise the need of knowledge of "The Gita" for kids, especially younger age group-school and college going generation so that they can enrich their lives with cultural and traditional heritage and values which generally lack in the present era in normal upbringing routines of many Indian families.

- For this , I especially request the great parents to introduce "The Gita" as a healthy, friendly, easy and holy scripture to their kids and that it should be their First Spiritual Guide and Friend!

- As the challenges of building better responsible Indian citizens grows day by day, so is the need to spread a word about such easily available and valuable scriptures like "The Gita" the prime essence of today's era.

- It should be well understood that the guidelines and teachings of "The Gita" are not obsolete, rather they work perfectly and go hand in hand with every unknown new troubles emerging in our lives.

- Finally, there is no better literature scripture Book available for guidance, hope, help, company and strength than "The Gita"!!

Afterword

Thanks for reading and making up
this far!
Hope this book resolved your queries and bursted
your myths about the learnings and preachings
Of the great scripture: "THE GITA"
And the book served your
expectations and purpose!
You can freely learn Geeta on
https://www.learngeeta.com
You can also subscribe to my
different social media like Twitter,
Instagram, Facebook and Youtube.
And once again, don't forget to
subscribe for my E-Newsletter on
www.ispharmacologydifficult.com

****

Acknowledgements

I especially want to mention a vote of thanks first

and foremost to "GURUJI" whose learnings have

guided the making of this book and who has been an

invisible motivation behind every word of the book!

Secondly, a great thanks to my family, especially my

Aunt and my Mom

who unplanned gifted the trip to me!

And next, my son who is always interested in my

books and this serves as a catalyst to my writing

ventures!!

Next a great thanks to my brother for always being

there by my side through the thick and thin!

And never to forget , heartiest thanks to you all, the

spiritually curious devotees and clan!

"You are the best!"

****

About The Author

DR RADHIKA VIJAY ,

MBBS, MD Pharmacology

belongs to Bikaner, Rajasthan, India.

She is a faculty in Sardar Patel Medical College, Bikaner. She

has always been an elite

student since her school days. She has been teaching

Medical Pharmacology for the last 10 years now!!

Appreciator of everything brilliant and intelligent in life and

with an optimistic

attitude and approach she believes

in the value and power of time, prayers and purpose

driven consistency as strong foundation elements in one's

life!!

You can connect:

Personal Website - https://www.drradhikavijay.com

Podcast Website: https://www.ispharmacologydifficult.com

Twitter : https://twitter.com/IsPharmacology

Instagram:

https://www.instagram.com/ispharmacologydifficult/

Youtube:

https://www.youtube.com/channel/UC-LnUrZKlcBuQaLa2

HDQOVg